FINISHING LINE PRESS

www.finishinglinepress.com

Edisonia

poems by

Richard Thomas Murray

Finishing Line Press
Georgetown, Kentucky

Edisonia

Publisher: Leah Huete de Maines
Editor: Christen Kincaid
Author Photo: Maria Knapp
Cover Design: Elizabeth Maines McCleavy

Order online: www.finishinglinepress.com
also available on amazon.com

Author inquiries and mail orders:
Finishing Line Press
P. O. Box 1626
Georgetown, Kentucky 40324
U. S. A.

Table of Contents

For Erica

The temple bell fades
But the flowers keep ringing
Into the evening.

—Basho
(Translated from the Japanese by Richard Jones)

To suffer any toil, to keep my watch
Through the still nights, seeking the words, the song
Whereby to bring your mind that splendid light
By which you can see darkly hidden things.

—Lucretius, from The Way Things Are
(Translated from the Latin by Rolfe Humphries)

Practical Invocation

Inventors must be poets
so that they may have imagination.
—Thomas Edison

Wizard of Menlo Park,
I realize our connections
sound like inexact science,
but I'm not making this up:
a 2/11 birthdate equals
our mutual patent number;
and I'm addressing you
from the town bearing your name
that I call home,
spot you put on the map
when you brought the sun down
to Earth on it
and didn't get burned,
turned nights into days
and made the world
shine like something new.

I'm not asking you
to help me become a luminary
with a magical name like yours,
or rich from poetry
since words are cheap.
Let's coordinate our efforts
to make this poem
and all that follow
more than literary devices,
put our heads together
to speak with a hybrid voice
and get creative about being practical.
Connect the veins wiring my body
for sound to music
beyond the range of human ears.
Collaborate with me to turn lines

of words into filaments
on more than a metaphorical level,
electrified by a current
that burns them alive
and illuminates this manuscript.

Speaking of light bulbs,
they're all off in my neighborhood
at this late hour,
except for the white-hot skull
turning my brain into more
than a gray area.

Protective Measures

You feel it catch
in the skeletal net.
Muscles get a grip.
Veins tie it down.
Skin holds it in.

It opens your eyes
to the tangled message
hazel branches inscribe
across the peeled face
of the apple moon
papering the horizon.

White birch filaments
illuminate the invisible.
Stakes made of ash
raise your solid house
above drowning in it.
A willow moat
guards against fire.

The Tree of Light

Reading between the lines
of an illuminated manuscript
projected onto the wall
through the open blinds
of an unlit room
reveals the flowering dogwood
wired to the ground
outside the glittering window
its white bulbs electrified
moonlight turning them up
to a higher power.

Deja Vu Variations

The color turned local
when I recognized my hometown,
miniaturized inside my television
as though I were seeing it
from the distance of twenty years.
Its Victorian preservations
reconstructed the scene
for a film set
even further back in the past,
circa World War One.
Remembering my way around
before I was born there
was an imitation deja vu feeling.

I viewed this fake reappearance
as a sign to go back
in more real time,
which I made with the foot
I put to the pedal.
That single step accelerated my return
so past and present blurred
by the time I arrived at
where I'd come from,
an effect I'm remembering
in the foreseeable future.

Sculpture Garden

If environment really has a hand
in molding personality,
how did it figure
in what's fashionably known
as an impressionable youth
on an island shaped like a huge fish?
Does it explain a feel for undercurrents?
Why I swim in circumstances
where other people sink?
And what formed the image of Long Island
in such perfect scale
is an even deeper question.
Thousands chiseled features
on the face of Rushmore;
one Korczak Ziolkowski
cut almost everything else
out of his life
to identify a whole South Dakota mountain
with Chief Crazy Horse.
Was it artistic nature
that shaped the larger-than-life profile
of Owl's Head Mountain?
And if the moon is a statuesque face
worn beyond recognition,
who carved it,
and what great face hung over us?

Thomas Edison's Apocalyptic Novel

He threw an asteroid at us
from the darkest space
in his fictional mind,
which cut us out
of the plot he was convinced
would sell to millions
of the would-be extinct.

But nobody bought it
because it was never published,
its unfinished state the main reason
Edison's sci-fi novel
still has no future.
Add a plot device
not inventive enough because it borrowed
too much from Jules Verne:
we're replaced by a human element
that walks in water,
though Edison didn't tell the story
of how they got down there,
another flaw to fix;
so's their gilded civilization,
a too-perfect defect.

Putting an eleven-foot-wide telescope
into the hands of those characters
was a novel idea.
It enlarged their vision
to include a delegation of extraterrestrials
heading in their direction
for what they'd signaled
would be a dialogue
Edison didn't include a word of,
maybe saving that for a sequel.

Jersey Shore Summers

It was no marina act:
dolphins grounded on our beaches
weren't playing dead.
And we didn't pretend
to know why,
wondered if they were so smart
they knew something about the future
that drove them to mass suicide.
But in the immediate future,
scientists sized-up
a cause of death
more down-to-earth:
microscopic human shit
from the dumping grounds
not far enough off
Sandy Hook.
The foaming ocean
had been giving us
the same shit for weeks,
confining our suspect asses
to the increasing heat
of scratchy beaches.
That was last summer's news.
This year, heavy doses
of vials and syringes
washing up have cured
even the beaches of crowds.
We're beginning to disappear from everywhere.

Why You Shouldn't Buy a House in the Dismal Swamp

That area will always be
the Dismal Swamp
to anyone native,
even though a sign
calling it Paradise Acres
is carved in stone.
A thousand streetlights
won't brighten it up,
bring into focus
what's blurred by fog
nearly every night.
It's mainly wetlands
so perpetual dampness
weighs down, depresses
the very atmosphere
and gets into everything,
even your head.
If those aren't reasons enough:
endangered marsh hawks
might mistake your hair
for something to eat;
raccoons will rip apart your garbage,
may not stop at that;
and if you're superstitious,
disturbed Lenape bones
will attack your imagination.
Scratch yourself from the buyer list
if you don't like mosquitoes;
or neighbors who won't speak to you
because you could never be as quiet
as 500 acres of wilderness,
and because no matter how good-looking,
you could never compete with a view
that's anything but dismal.
Such extensive background
increases the visibility of the stars,
seems to enlarge the moon

and makes us feel
closer to the universe.
An astronomer or a minister
moving into our midst
couldn't do that for us.

Lenape Submarine

A whitened human skull
rose like a periscope
from waves of churned-up dirt
where construction disturbed more
than just the neighbors
with its noisy machinery.
Fixed in its sights,
a sinking feeling shot through me.

Photographic Memory

for Jeffrey Lang
and in memory of Herman Lang,
U.S. Army Photographer at the Dachau Concentration Camp, 1945

When we look up
from your grandfather's album
riddled with camp shots,
our breathing sounds like people running.
He captured kids around our age
who couldn't get out
of the pictures we can escape
by closing the book.

Glam Dicinn

"What good's this shit?"
it hears you complaining
about my other poems
it's very attached to,
spread out before you
instead of the valuables
fireproof boxes usually contain.
That's a reasonable question
for a thief to be asking
since everybody knows poetry doesn't pay.
Poems don't make anything happen either,
according to W.H. Auden,
a twentieth-century practitioner.
People in the more distant past
believed a good poem
jumped off the page
in a different way
than we mean that
as a compliment today.
Sometimes they'd declare it
a glam dicinn, nonsense in English
that's curse poem in their language.
This one teaches you a lesson.

Tenth Spring

The flowering white dogwood
demands a trimming
scratches onto the window
etched into my memory
the transparent story
of its branches
covered with pieces
of shredded moon
that passed too close
in the swollen night
leaving me to wonder
what it wrote there.

The Honorable Jane Byrne

That's how the first woman mayor
of Chicago was introduced,
but the Jane Byrne
I'm presenting to you
was my eighty-year-old neighbor
in a different city.

She summoned me into her apartment
from the shadow of a hallway
our slumlord hadn't painted
in over thirty years
to unveil an urban renewal project
she announced was personal
because she'd funded it
with the last of her money.

Glossy paint like new skin
surrounded her reincarnated spirit
in every room she showed off,
and polished floors created a platform
for her to walk in light,
as did the gleam
of new appliances generating a buzz
in that charged atmosphere.

The winning smile plastered
like a poster on her face
inspired my votive support
as she paraded around that apartment
like she owned it,
empowered to consider herself
one of the elect.

On the Invention of a Device for Capturing the Voices of Spirits

> *...if there are personalities in another existence or*
> *sphere who wish to get in touch with us in this existence or*
> *sphere, the apparatus will at least give them a better*
> *opportunity to express themselves than the tilting tables and*
> *raps and ouija boards and mediums and other crude methods."*
> *—Thomas Edison*
> *(from Scientific American magazine, circa 1920)*

1.

A different spin on your phonograph
never materialized into even a prototype.
No record of it
in a single notebook
built it up into a fabrication.
It haunted a seance in 1941
when you voiced complaints
about assistants ghosting everything
to solidify your reputation
in the hard sciences
instead of the occult.
Thinking about an apparatus
equated in your mind
to tinkering with it,
so maybe you made it work
and heard voices in your head
the same way you're registering mine
through this reverse mechanism.

2.

Reinventing myself as ghostwriter
turns this poetic device
for capturing my voice
into my opus posthumous

my patent number 1,094
even though your name
is all over it.
It works on more than paper

to bring this message
through the wired ears
coiling into your head.
They twist my words
into language you understand
in no uncertain terms.

Santa Claus

His father told us
he recognized the irony
of a Jew looking like Santa Claus
when he identified the body
he hadn't seen in twenty years,
a mythical figure also
to the Queens neighbors
who rarely saw him
come down to Earth
from his high-rise apartment,
where he'd stay up all night
on the thirtieth floor
in a confusing astrology
of stars and lights
he didn't know how to chart;
where he ate himself
into someone larger than life,
and withheld his many gifts
from the human race.

George Merkle

His record-setting speed
in high school track
left his name behind
in the trophy case,
and the clairvoyant body
that matured way ahead of schedule
beat all of us
to the fastest girls.
Acceleration was a pattern
kept up to the finish line
of his crash-course life,
which flashed before his wide-open eyes
at a hundred miles an hour.

In Memory of My Middle Name

Few know it's there
after the first name
we rarely get beyond
unless it's to go
directly to my surname.
It usually comes out
only in legal documents
untrained eyes never see,
or when family relate
how that name went through another
to get to me.
Shortened to a T.,
it's a sign of the cross
over all that remains
of the paratrooper who had Thomas
shot out of him
as he came down to Earth
like a puppet with cut strings.

Life Size

Body chemistry couldn't alchemize
age-old, basic truth,
and make golden years
out of the transformation
of a man not in his element.
His violin in his stiffening hands
felt like dead wood
that rang hollow and echoed troubles
not music to his tin ears.
Iron-poor blood and metal fatigue
of steel nerves had him leaning
toward a complete collapse,
yet he seemed more inclined
to not cave in
the last time I saw him standing.
His overly firm handshake
gave the impression of someone trying
too hard to hold on,
and revealed a statue
he was turning into
from the inside out,
starting with the hardening of his arteries.

Illuminations

The miles we travelled
to our local hospital and back
equalled the usual trip
to the Lakes Region.
Our view was jaundiced
instead of scenic then,
our father's panoramic face
a highlighted passage for future tests.

I can't enlighten you
about what my sister sees inside
her burned-out head,
but I saw through the smoke
who was burning to get lit
for what felt like an eternity.
I was his afterlife.
That was hell too.

Water Spirit

for Olaf Olsen

No riddle at all:
two-thirds of him
was made of it.
He broke his mother's
to land in this world,
which he sailed around
a total of seven times
as though to dilute it.
He later built a life
around the shipyards
of fish-shaped Long Island,
and never lived out of
hearing range of the sea,
his ears miniature shells.
The day water filled his lungs
he was turning completely into it,
his rising temperature melting him
until he couldn't even stand.
The stormy brainwaves
flooding his consciousness
poured from his eyes
and blurred the line
between this world
and the next one.

Immortality

The patio furniture I left outside
this summer
is buried now in a grave
of snow level with the desk
from which I rise.

Theory of Evolution

It's at my fingertips,
where dry skin's splitting
from something bigger than I am
trying to reach beyond
me into the world
of flesh it wants to touch.
It will work its way out
of my ripped body
like an explorer who has crossed
the two-thirds of me that's water
to kneel and kiss
the solid ground it walks on.

Time Travelers

We lost our poses
in front of Cape May Victorians
we were about to go inside
and the ocean background
we never went into.
Yet that missing place
built up more than photographic memories,
its special preserve,
and gave landmark status
to a vacation that didn't last.
Lack of air conditioning
and tidal heat wave
combined to make us go back
two days before it was time
to turn ourselves around,
as did a discomfort less physical
but felt even more.
We couldn't recreate our past life
before the presence of the baby
left behind with family.
We kept coming back to her
in our idle conversation,
itself a thing of the past.

Hippie Presence in Goa, India

Dust looked like smoke
as she drifted out of it,
her face lighting up
a tie-dyed dress
like a silent explosion
in the vindaloo air.
The flashback burned out
when her wide-open smile
didn't have any teeth in it.

After An Argument

Darkness weighs on me
like a giant period,
yet I can't get any deeper
than lying still,
a flat-out imitation
of the sleep I'm so conscious of
being unable to realize.
The whites of my eyes like moons
are my worst enemies,
but I could also mention
an invisible foe:
blasts of heat
venting right in my face,
from the fired-up furnace
that's been making noise all night.
My pillow also doesn't muffle
the yelling I can't get
out of my head,
nor does it soften my anger
toward the person sleeping beside me,
who irritates me so well
she can do it
even with her eyes closed.

Photographic Evidence

They'd noticed tourists draping an arm
around each other's shoulders
as though hugging with one hand
tied behind our backs,
making love look easy
said the newlyweds we bonded with
in the plaza outside their church.
But they didn't recognize
how foreign we were
from what we appeared to be,
nor how much we didn't fit
into the wedding photo
they insisted on squeezing us into
until our gritted teeth
were mistaken for smiles
as the camera clicked.

Freak Storm

At its furthest point
from where we're grounded
at a high elevation,
the sun's too weak
to reach inside us
and melt what's hardened
even though it's July,
or take dim views
out of the way
we see each other
with our heads in the clouds
and sparks of snow
like breaking-up stars
coming down around us,
more glitter than substance.

Mix-Ups

Everything that year
out of place:
drought hardened
our emotional walls
into physical ones
at separate addresses;
dried-up trees
made fall appear
way ahead of schedule,
their inflamed leaves
adding to record heat
at the same time.

Then summer flared again
in the early fall,
raised dead air
to the temperature
of a human body,
alive with the sexual scent
of warmed-up, decaying leaves
like arrows scattered
all over the ground
and hanging over our heads,
pointing everywhere
to a connection
between love and death.

Haunted by our bodies,
we came to a standstill
under an empty tree,
the tangled shadow
of its branches
tying us to each other
every bit as much
as the weight of this embrace.

Sexual Hieroglyphics

The acts they depicted
were expected to translate
into language coming alive
in the third dimension
where I'm picturing in my head
animated people like us
having off-the-wall sex,
a graphic fantasy words turn physical
as soon as you get here.

The True Father of Rock and Roll

Variations on Edison's phonograph
are hits with me
wherever they turn up.
I raise my volume
to tune out other people's radios
stationary beside me in traffic jams
and at red lights,
or a person who won't stop
yakety-yakking from my passenger seat
or inside my head.
I stuff headphones in my ears
for music when I'm in libraries
and when I jog,
and when I need a wall
of sound between me
and other human beings
or hearing myself think.
But listen, registering my vocal appreciation
doesn't require toning down my criticism.
If Edison were here right now,
I'd give that half-deaf bastard
an earful about the noisy world
he was instrumental in creating,
where my neighbor's rock and roll
at sky-high volume
drowns out the birds
when I open windows
not to mention breezes
anything but dead air.

Mixed-Up Odyssey

Twenty years of marriage
took me to places
I couldn't get out
of my wandering mind,
where I was turned
into something I'm not
even after the magic wore off.

I stuffed my ears
with my own voice
to hear myself think
while I was tied in knots
to the mast of my bones
in a journey rigged against me.

I took deep breaths
to steady my brainwaves
so they wouldn't drown my eyes,
which opened my skin
into a sail that carried me
into arms that feel like home
wherever we may be.

Night Shift

My body feels dislocated
by a rural environment
where the absence of light pollution
litters the sky with more stars
than I've ever seen
in my personal space.
It's not in sync
with a foreign timezone
where my hosts are all asleep
while I'm not dreaming
I notice the Big Dipper
like a crack in the window,
tilted so it's filling
my lit-up eyes
with the fuel of the stars.

Historical Footnote

There has not been a double burial found in the
Neolithic period, much less two people
hugging—and they really are hugging.
—Elena Menotti
Archaeologist, 2007

When we dusted them
off enough to recognize
a couple hugging in their grave,
those bones were runes
we didn't know how to interpret.
Then we observed the sunlight glittering
with particles we'd stirred up,
a giant asterisk around the site.

Acknowledgments

Grateful acknowledgment is made to the editors of the following print publications in which some of these poems first appeared, a couple in slightly different form:

Albatross:
Jersey Shore Summers
Why You Shouldn't Buy a House in the Dismal Swamp

The Bitter Oleander:
Protective Measures
The Tree of Light
Tenth Spring

The Broome Review:
Mix-Ups (formerly Indian Summer)

Connecticut River Review:
Sculpture Garden

The Moth:
Immortality

Poetry East:
Historical Footnote
In Memory of My Middle Name

Rattle:
After an Argument

Santa Fe Literary Review:
Santa Claus

Slipstream:
Theory of Evolution
Life Size

Small Pond:
Water Spirit

Richard Thomas Murray received his B.A. from Goddard College in Vermont where he studied with Louise Gluck (informally), Marvin Bell, Ellen Bryant Voigt, Barry Goldensohn, Lorrie Goldensohn, and Paul Nelson. He received his M.A. in English (Creative Writing Concentration) from Rutgers University-Newark where he studied with Rachel Hadas and John A. Williams. His poems have appeared in a number of national and international literary journals including *The Moth, Slipstream, The Bitter Oleander, Poetry East,* and *Rattle.* He has taught creative writing at Rutgers University-New Brunswick since 2007. He has also been an activist for New Jersey's three major Native American tribes, and was responsible for their being the featured community at the 2018 New Jersey Folk Festival that starred the Apsaalooke hip-hop artist and rapper Supaman.

www.ingramcontent.com/pod-product-compliance
Lightning Source LLC
Chambersburg PA
CBHW031220090426
42740CB00009B/1249